Caught in the Middle

A letter to my divorced parents

Benjamin D. Garber, PhD

Publisher's Note

This publication is designed to provide accurate and
authoritative information about the subject matters covered.
It is sold with the understanding that neither the publisher
nor the author are rendering legal, mental health, or other
professional services in this book. If expert assistance, legal
services or counseling is needed before making decisions that
impact you, your children and your family, the services of a
competent professional should be sought.

In writing this book, gender-specific pronouns and roles such
as "Mom" or "Dad" are used. Please do not let these references
confuse you. There is nothing in this book that is exclusively
true of any gender, sexual orientation or caregiving role. For
simplification purposes, the family in this book has only one
child; however, everything discussed in the book is relevant to
families with multiple children, allowing for the complications
of understanding and serving the children's unique needs.

ISBN 9781950057221

Copyright © 2018 by Benjamin D. Garber

Unhooked Books, LLC 7701 E. Indian School Rd., Ste. F
Scottsdale, AZ 85251 www.unhookedbooks.com

Library of Congress Control Number: 2018953502

Book design: Julian Leon, The Missive
Printed in the United States of America

Contents

To my parents,

Now that I finally graduated, you asked me what growing up in our family was like...

...At first I didn't want
to think about how
hard things have been.

Not just the divorce. ←
That was **just a date**
on the calendar.

Looking back, my
whole childhood seems
to be about your
~~fights.~~

I know that there
were some good times,
but they all seemed to
be stained by the **bad**.

Divorce Doesn't Harm Children. Parents Do.

Divorce is just a legal piece of paper.

It can be as unemotional as filing taxes or as traumatic as being sentenced to life in prison.

The fact is that you don't have to be married to have children, and you don't have to divorced to harm them.

Never-married couples, single parents, same-sex parents, intergenerational co-parents, married and even divorced parents can raise healthy children.

The legal status of the adult relationship doesn't matter. What matters is how adults who share responsibility for a child cooperate and communicate and work together to serve that child's needs.

Adults who cannot manage these basics risk harming their child by leaving them caught in the middle.

I'm old enough
now to be able to
say that I love you
both.

I don't have to
choose sides, but
I'm still mad and sad
and confused.

I remember the bad
times as far back as
memory can go.

Maybe by sharing her journal, Emma can help you learn to raise healthier children.

This book is written for adult consumption.

This is Emma's journal, a fictitious 18-year-old high school graduate who grew up in the middle of her parents' selfish war.

It's important that you not mistake Emma for every child of divorced parents. In fact, the vast majority of parents who separate and divorce are healthy and mature.

They are able to put their past behind them, to put their kids' needs first, and go on to raise healthy kids.

They are able to learn to communicate and cooperate. They find ways to establish consistent parenting practices.

They establish a schedule of care that suits their specific child's very specific needs and, when problems arise, they are able to enlist skilled, trusted, child-centered professionals to help them over the bumps in the road.

Emma's experience as documented in this book is very different.

Emma is an amalgam of hundreds of children.

Children that I have known who found themselves caught in the middle of their parents' conflicts. The rage and narcissistic injuries that these parents live with day-to-day blind them to their children's needs.

As a result, children like Emma are prematurely thrust into the adult world. They are forced to become their parents' allies and confederates, messengers and spies. They give up their childhoods in order to serve their parents' selfish needs.

They become chameleons, changing who they are in order to fit into the adult world, or ostriches, burying their heads in the sands of denial.

Emma's done a very selfless thing by sharing this journal with you. The thoughts and feelings that she shares here are very private. Even embarrassing. But Emma and I have decided to put this book in your hands in the singular hope that maybe you will make different choices than her parents did.

I know that some
children fall asleep
in their cribs to the
sound of lullabies.
I used to fall asleep
to the sound of your
arguments.

I remember feeling
scared.

It doesn't even
matter whether
I was old enough
to understand
the words.

But They're Too Young to Understand!

Don't fool yourself. Our kids read our emotions and body language

They hear the beat of our hearts and the pace of our breathing, they sense the hormones associated with love and rage, fear and sadness, long before they learn language. Long before they understand our words.

An infant can tell if the adult holding him or her is nervous or confident, and they respond in kind. An infant held firmly in the arms of a calm caregiver is more likely to settle.

That baby's happy smiles and cooing, reassure the caregiver, who will think, "What a sweet baby" or "I'm good at this!" or "she loves me so much!"

The child, in turn, will read the caregiver's growing pleasure and feel happier herself, on and on and on, in a perpetual feedback loop of emotions.

But it works the other way, too.

A baby held in the arms of an anxious caregiver will read that anxiety more easily than you are reading this page. The caregiver's anxiety will fuel the child's brewing distress. As the baby begins to fuss, the caregiver will become more anxious.

The tone of your voices, the tenseness of your bodies when you held me, even your **BOOM-BOOM-BOOM** heartbeat when you tried to comfort me all left me feeling bruised and exhausted.

So I'd cry. But my crying only made it worse.

Maybe that's why I never cry anymore.

She'll think, *"What's wrong with her?"* or *"What am I doing wrong?"* or *"She doesn't love me!"* which revs up the baby's fussiness.

Now imagine how this parent-child dynamic plays out against the back-drop of adult conflict, separation or divorce. Dad is frustrated after an argument with Mom when he goes to pick up the baby. The baby reads his upset in his racing heart and rapid, shallow breathing and responds in kind. Dad doesn't have the patience for a fussing baby—not after what happened with Mom—and thinks, *"Oh great! So you hate me, too?"* or *"I can't even do this right!"* Or Mom sees the baby fussing in Dad's arms and complains, *"You're hurting our daughter!"*

Get the picture? Growing up day after day, year after year, in that environment is like growing up in a war zone.

Across development, that baby's **brain chemistry**

becomes measurably different than the brain chemistry of her twin raised in a calm and loving home. Her cortisol levels—the brain chemical associated with fight or flight responses—are higher. She lives constantly on yellow alert. She can devote fewer cognitive resources to learning and growing, making friends and playing sports.

She's more likely to withdraw or act out, to become depressed and/or angry.

Science has taught us that children caught in the middle of their parents' persistent conflicts are at high risk for serious mental health problems, underachievement and school failure, run-away, drug and alcohol abuse, and for repeating these same destructive patterns of relationships as adults.

But science tends to be abstract and technical, it is weighted down by ten-syllable words and indecipherable statistics.

I believe that if we really want to help parents make different choices—that if we really want to raise a healthier next generation—then we need a compelling, first-person narrator to tell this story.

Emma has volunteered.

You thought I was
asleep, but I heard
everything.

I heard the swearing
and the threats.
I heard the doors slam
and the dishes break.

I heard the
promises broken.

Kids Always Blame Themselves

They might not admit it, but it's true of all of us deep down inside.

Long into adulthood, that primitive, irrational idea persists despite all logic to the contrary, even after years of therapy.

"It was my fault that my Dad abused me" or *"If I had been a better student, my mother wouldn't have left"* or *"I was just four-years-old, but I should have known better... they broke up because of me."*

Perhaps this is evolution's way of protecting us? It's easy to imagine that a child who blames her parents and distances herself from Mom and Dad is more vulnerable to being eaten by the next sabretooth tiger to wander by.

A child who blames herself and remains near Mom and Dad will be protected from predators and might live to reproduce, passing down her self-blaming genes to you and me.

don't lie

I used to make promises, too.
Silly little-kid promises.
don't lie

I promised to brush my teeth
and do my homework and eat
my vegetables
...if the fighting would stop.
don't lie

I promised to do my chores
...if you'd stop yelling.
don't lie

I promised to be the best kid
in the world and get good
grades and always...
don't lie

Is guilt built into our DNA?

I have worked as a child and family therapist, Guardian ad litem, custody evaluator and expert witness for over thirty years. I have known thousands of children who have grown up like Emma, caught in the middle of their parents' selfish war.

At some point along the course of development, **every single one of them has made a magical deal with him- or herself,** as if something that the child is doing or not doing is the cause of the adult conflict.

"If I get straight As in school..."
"If I'm nice to my sister..."
"If I take care of Mommy ...."
"If I don't get Daddy mad...."

Knowing this fact about your kids can help you be a better parent.

1 **Don't lie. Lies will only get you through the Moment.**
They will inevitably come back around and make things worse. Lies destroy trust. Trust is the safety net that allows our children to feel confident and secure.

2 **Insulate your children as much as you can.**
Protecting them from harsh realities is not lying, it's your job as a caregiver. Whether the issue is adult substance abuse, mental illness or disability, the family's economic struggles, or the adults' marital conflict, there is a great deal that the kids do not need to know.

3 **Reassure honestly and with insight:**
"Mom and Dad are working on it as best as we can" and *"it's not your fault"* and *"your job is to be a kid."*

4 **Listen for the emotion hiding behind the obvious content in your kids' questions.**
For example, the first best answer to, *"Why are you guys arguing?"* is NOT that Dad is a jerk and there's not enough money to buy groceries and that you're seriously depressed. The first best answer is to acknowledge the child's implicit emotion: *"You sound scared, sweetie. Do you need a hug?"* or *"This is pretty confusing, I bet."*

5 **Take care of yourself.**
Your healthy diet, regular exercise, and time with supportive friends is all to your kids' benefit. Community and connections are key. Isolating will make the problem worse. Get up, get out, and get talking.

I said that even the
good times feel "stained"
in my memory.

Remember
"happy meal Tuesdays"?

You said that if you didn't
have to cook
and do dishes one day a
week, things would
get better.

Put the Child's Needs First

If you love your child more than you hate the other parent, **then you will take the high road**. If you love your child more than you hate the other parent, then you'll put your own anger and fear and adult needs on the back burner.

If you love your daughter (or son) more than you hate her other parent, then you'll do everything in your power to assure that her needs come first.

Rituals are **emotional anchors** that make the world predictable.

Emma's parents made a superficial effort by creating "Happy Meal Tuesdays." They had the right idea: Let's create a weekly family ritual that we can all look forward to.

When they go well, rituals can help kids get through the hard times by looking forward to something in the future that they know will be easier.

But Emma's parents couldn't do it. They let their conflict leak into "Happy Meal Tuesdays."

Like everything else in Emma's life, the ritual became contaminated with anger and conflict. What might have been a reassuring weekly family event, became just another opportunity to be exposed to Mom and Dad's selfish battles.

What failed?

We'd go out for a school night fast-food picnic...

It didn't work.

I don't think the three of us ever really had a happy meal.

Fair Warning

I want you to focus on your child and join her in her world, but you must not intrude. Different children at different ages will be more-or-less private. More-or-less guarded. Unless there's reason to fear that a child is in danger or engaged in dangerous activities, allow her a degree of privacy appropriate to her maturity.

This is especially important when parents live apart. **Your questions about her experience with her other parent and in that parent's home are likely to fuel her anxiety.** She may feel like she's betraying that parent, telling secrets, or being enlisted as your spy.

"Taking the high road" means:

Not taking the bait

It means not reacting to your adult partner when you think that he or she is provoking you. Taking the high road doesn't mean not talking. Your kids will feel the tension in the strained silence as clearly as they hear obscenities and slammed doors.

Taking the high road means genuinely letting the button-pushing zingers float by like so many leaves on a breezy autumn day. You're aware that they're there, but you pay no attention.

Focusing on your child

It means stepping out of yourself long enough to set aside the pressures and the rage and the worries so that you can engage her in her world. Do you know what's important to her?

What music does she like? Who are her friends? What is her favorite color? What does she watch on TV, YouTube? What video game does she like best? Can you join her in understanding her world?

Being aware of yourself

Focus on the problem you are trying to solve. Not criticizing the other person.

Be aware of yourself and where you tend to criticize the other person and away from solving problems, get back to solving problems.

Not only will these strategies help to keep the conflict from boiling over, when adult conflicts do erupt in front of the kids, they model healthy ways to manage strong emotions and solve problems.

I hated school,
and never wanted to go.

My teachers were always
telling me that I was so
smart. I should just "apply
myself" or "try harder."

Why couldn't they see?

Structure Reduces Anxiety

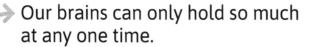 Our brains can only hold so much at any one time.

We human beings are very limited, finite creatures. The more emotion in the bottom of the cup, the less room is left for new information. But the opposite is true, too: The less emotion in the cup, the more room we have for learning.

A child who lives in chaos and conflict is forced to devote her very finite resources to basic survival skills. *Where will my next meal come from? How will I keep both of them happy at the same time? Who will be there to take care of me? What should I do next time Mom and Dad get in a fight?*

If I go with Dad this weekend, Mom will be mad. If I stay with Mom this weekend, Dad will be mad.

It's not reasonable to expect a child whose brain is overflowing with the fear and worry, anger and sadness, guilt and confusion to pay attention to algebra or chemistry or piano lessons.

And it's not a surprise that these children often refuse to go to school or the other parent's home, stay involved in sports (they are too overwhelmed). Some manufacture belly aches or headaches in order to stay home. Others simply refuse to leave the house.

Part of this may be genuine school avoidance.

Who wants to go somewhere that you feel stupid because you can't keep up? But part of this behavior is a fear of leaving home. Missing out.

It's really hard to care about 2+2 and verb conjugations when you don't know what's happening at home.

Mom + Dad = Fight

I never knew whether last night's threats were coming true, while my teacher droned on about history or science.

Mom + Dad = Fight

Paying attention when your world is falling apart is like trying to pour water into a cup that's already full.

Here's some clues to consider when your son or daughter is having trouble in school:

Structure reduces anxiety.
When getting up, traveling to school, and the school day itself are predictable A-B-C sequences of events, anxiety will diminish. Some of what's filling the cup will drain away so that there's more room for learning.

This means minimizing or eliminating unpredictables like which parent is present, which seat the child sits in on the bus, and what subject is taught first upon arrival.

Does this mean that children should always "launch" their school days from the same home? For some of the more anxious and rigid children, it does. For most children, however, it simply means that:

The schedule of care should be predictable so that the child knows *"if this is Thursday, then I'm at Daddy's house;"*

The sequence of events within each home should be predictable so that, *"if this is Daddy's house, then first I get dressed, next I eat a bowl of cereal, then I get my backpack and the bus comes at 7:15; and..."*

Ideally, the sequence of events should be the same in both homes so that the child doesn't need to think about it.

This consistency of parenting policies and practices is important for children in every situation, but especially when parents live apart.

Missing school on Tuesday will make getting to school on Wednesday ten times harder.

Unless a medical professional advises otherwise, it's always better to get your son or daughter to school today even it means an argument, even if she goes directly to the school nurse or counselor.

I was always tired.
My grades were falling.
I got in trouble a lot.
So Mom took me to
the doctor.

He meant well, I guess.
But doctors look inside
their patients for
problems. Maybe it's my
appendix? Or the flu?
Maybe my diet?

My problem wasn't
inside of me, at least
not at first.

Attention Deficit Hyperactivity Disorder

And other Childhood Psychiatric Illnesses

Here's how I ended up in family law: I worked in a busy child therapy clinic early in my career. For years I was astonished to find that seven or eight out of every ten children (especially boys) referred for child therapy were diagnosed with Attention Deficit Hyperactivity Disorder (ADHD).

It was true that these children couldn't concentrate, were highly distractible, and impulsive. But unless there was poison in the air or water, it just wasn't likely that so many children had the same illness.

ADHD is a very real illness that affects thinking, learning, relationships and behavior. There are very useful behavior therapies and medications for people with genuine ADHD. But you can't catch ADHD like the flu and you can't "get" ADHD by living in chaos and conflict.

When I started to look beyond the child-patient to understand the family, at least half of these "ADHD" kids were caught in the middle of their parents' conflicts. Their cups were full—like Emma's—so they couldn't pay attention.

A student who can't pay attention frequently gets criticized, punished and ridiculed. Self-esteem plummets. Anger and sadness are fueled. "Why bother?" is the result, so homework gets lost or forgotten or finished at home but never turned in.

The bus is missed, classes are skipped, and school refusal takes root. Social connections are made with other, similar kids who reinforce the angry, self-disparaging "why bother?" idea. You can see, perhaps, how this can lead down the road to underachievement, drugs and alcohol, sexual acting out, and trouble with the law.

At first my problem
was you. I know that
now. I woke up every
day in a war zone.

After school,
I rode the bus home to
the battle front.

The dinner table and the
TV room and even bath-
time were mine fields.

But those things
don't show up on
x-rays or blood tests.

I recognized that there's very little good done providing therapy one hour each week to a child when they go home to spend the other 167 hours each week immersed in chaos and conflict.

There is a place for diagnosis and medication, but we go there far too quickly. Just as Emma points out, the medical model fails us when it looks only within the patient for causes and solutions.

We must understand each patient—every child—as a whole person who exists within complex, dynamic systems of relationships.

Identifying a childlike Emma with a mental illness is worse than a diagnostic error.

The risk is that the label will give the entire family system a scapegoat (*"things are tense because our daughter has a problem!"*) and will validate Emma's deepest fears (*"It's my fault they're fighting. It's my ADHD."*)

So what's the answer?

Don't hesitate to seek professional assistance, but be an informed consumer and a strong advocate for your child. Choose providers carefully. Insist on meeting with the provider before bringing your child in for introductions so that you can ask questions and assure your child's comfort and safety.

1 **Ask about diagnoses in advance.**
How will diagnosis be determined? How will it be recorded? Can we talk about the diagnosis before it's communicated to your insurance company where it can become forever-after associated with the child's name?

2 **Make sure that the provider understands the child as part of the family system.**
In the case of psychotherapy ("counseling") this probably means adding parent and/or family meetings to the usual child meetings.

3 **But what does "family" mean when parents live apart?**
For many children, it's important to be clear that there are two families: one with Mom and one with Dad. Make sure that the child's provider recognizes this and understands the child's experience in both families.

So the doctor diagnosed
me with ADHD and said
that a pill would help.

Did the medicine help?
I guess we'll never know.

The medicine became
another thing
to argue about.

That proved what I'd
been thinking for years:
I was the problem.
If it weren't for me, you
wouldn't be arguing.

Therapy and Medication?

If you can't drain the pool, **get a life preserver!**

I think of children who live in the midst of adult conflict like swimmers in deep water. No matter how strong or practiced they are, their arms and legs will eventually tire and they're at risk of drowning.

Of course, some of these young swimmers are carrying other physical and genetic and behavioral weights that threaten to pull them under, but we really can't understand or respond to these needs completely while they're busy trying to keep their heads above water.

What's the first best choice? **Get them out of the water.**

That means ending the adult conflict. Establishing healthy, child-centered communication, cooperation and consistency of parenting practices.

Please notice that this does not necessarily mean healing the intimate adult relationship. Yes, that can help, but it's not necessary. The intimate adult relationship (meaning marriage, in many cases) can stop. **The co-parenting relationship must not.**

If it weren't for me, you guys would have been happy.

That's why I ran away freshman year. I figured if I was gone, you two would get along better.

If you didn't?

At least I wouldn't have to hear it any more.

And if you can't get the child out of the deep water?

If the adult conflict is so deeply entrenched and longstanding and bitter that none of these or other, similar remedies can help?

Then the next best choice is to give the child as many flotation devices and swimming lessons as possible.

This is when a skilled child therapist can be involved to support the child, careful not to get pulled into the adult battle.

School counselors, school- and community-based support groups can help, as well. In particular, helping the child find a niche of any kind where she feels successful and valued and competent outside the homes can sometimes be far more important than any therapy.

How can you fix a broken co-parenting relationship?

1 **Co-parenting therapy.**
This is not to be confused with marriage therapy. Co-parenting therapy is a nuts-and-bolts, practical and often educational process focused explicitly on communication, cooperation and consistency. Who should go? Take the high road. Put aside your anger and jealousy and resentment. Any adult who is actively engaged in caring for the child should participate.

Yes, this might mean your ex's new girlfriend or boyfriend or mother or roommate.

2 **Alternating family therapies with one therapist.**
One week Dad and the kids go. The next week Mom and the kids go. The mental health professional's job is to help the adults to establish healthy roles and rules within each family group and consistency and communication between the family groups.

3 **Parenting Coordination.**
A court-ordered process requiring the adults to work with a specially trained professional whose job is to resolve child-centered conflicts within the parameters of the existing parenting plan. The Parenting Coordinator (known by other names in some jurisdictions) is enabled by the court to determine the outcome of any particular matter if education and mediation fail.

4 **Mediation and arbitration.**
Alternative means of settling a dispute by impartial persons without proceeding to a court trial. It is sometimes preferred as a means of settling a matter in order to avoid the expense, delay, and acrimony of litigation.

5 **Lawyers and court?**
Conventional courts function on a guilty-innocent, good guy-bad guy basis and can make family matters worse. If you have access to a "family court" or a "child-centered court" you might find the process quicker, less expensive and more effective. In particular, look into whether you can find specially trained collaborative law attorneys.

When the cops brought
me home the next day,
I was tired and hungry
and scared.

You were so
busy blaming
each other, no one even
asked where I'd been.

Obviously, this requires timely,
child-centered and constructive
adult communication.

Dad said it was Mom's
fault because of
all the doctors and
the medicine and over-
protectiveness.

"We" Messages

"We" communicates that the parents are working together. It reassures the child that regardless of the idea being communicated, whether its good news or bad news, there is always a safety net there to catch her if she stumbles or falls. "We" requires that adults who share responsibility for a child—co-parents—talk together and reach an agreement before either of them talk to the child.

Struggling to communicate with your child's other parent?

1
You are no longer ex-partners.
You are now co-CEOs of the company named [insert child's name here]. Communicate with your co-parent the same way that you would communicate with a co-worker or the boss: polite, respectful and business-focused.

2
Make the timing of non-emergency communications predictable.
For example, plan a Thursday evening call after your daughter's in bed.

3
Make the content of the communication predictable.
Email an agenda to each other in advance. Agenda items must be child-centered, phrased without blame or shame, and succeedable. Succeedable means that it is possible to identify real life solutions, even if you might not agree on them. By contrast, *"why are you a jerk?"* meets none of these criteria.

4
Written communications often minimize the risk of misleading tone and body language.
Consider text messages or email, keeping in mind that email allows you to keep a record of communications for future reference, whereas text messages (and Tweets and Instagram and...) all disappear.

X Mom said it was
Dad's fault because
he was never there
and he obviously
didn't love us.

+ Dad said he'd show
her what it was like
to never be there.

That's when
he ran away.

But you called it
"divorce."

It means that all but the most mundane questions are first answered with *"I'll talk to your Dad, and WE will let you know."*

"We" messages are nowhere more important than when you tell the kids that you're separating or divorcing. Disappearing in the middle of the night or while the child's at school with no explanation is enough to fuel a lifetime of fears.

Face the music.
Take the high road.

If you love your child more than you hate her other parent, you'll talk together about what to say, how and where to say it:

1 Make it simple and brief.
Be there and be prepared for when she comes back to you with questions.

2 No blame, no matter how you see the facts.
"WE have decided to make a change" rather than *"Your Mom is leaving us."*

3 Don't be defensive.
Expect and validate strong feelings:
"You're right. I'm sure this makes you mad!"

4 Tell her together if you can.
Pick a time and day when she has some options about how to cope with the news. Just before bedtime and on her way out the door to school are mistakes. Supper time Saturday night? Brunch on Sunday morning? Either gives her some leeway to cope and gives you the opportunity to be there for her.

5 Make it concrete and predictable.
"Daddy's moving out in three days. He has an apartment near your school" is far better than *"sometime in the spring."*

6 Let her control what she can.
Can she help with packing? Can she choose the color of the walls in her room at the other house? These seeming little details help kids feel less helpless as the earth shifts beneath their feet.

I didn't understand.
I guess I still don't.

It doesn't even
matter how old I
was when Dad left.

My brain knows that
divorce happens,
but my heart felt
like a piece of the
inside of me was
being ripped out.

Emotions Aren't Logical

Our feelings don't have to make sense.
They often seem to be contradictory and changing and crazy.

It's normal and natural and very confusing to have many different feelings all at once, especially in response to powerful events. News that your parents are divorcing is about as big as it gets for most children, so it's realistic to expect that the news will trigger happiness and sadness, anger and fear all at once. The flood of relief and grief, shame and blame, terror and joy can be overwhelming. Your job is not to correct or criticize or even to add your feelings into the mix.

Your job is to support and be there for her, to help her understand one bite-sized portion at a time, so that she can better cope with the change.

Simply putting feelings into words is helpful. *"You seem really mad"* and *"I know that you're scared"* and *"I bet you're really, really sad right now"* all can help your kids label their feelings. Words do for feelings what bags do for groceries: They package them up so that we can more easily carry them around and share them with others.

And emotions can interfere with mature functioning. If you think about growing up like moving up a flight of stairs, most people have one foot forward testing out a new step, and one foot back, resting solidly on a familiar step. When emotion strikes, the first thing we do is pull back that forward foot. The energy that was invested in trying out new things has to be used for coping with feelings. The day after learning that your parents are divorcing is not the time to start in a new school, to try to learn a new skill or even to try a new vegetable.

I felt like I wanted
to stay home with
Mom AND I wanted
to go with Dad.

I was **SO MAD** at
Daddy for leaving
and **RELIEVED** that
he was gone.

If the feelings are huge or long-lasting, our next response is to begin backing down the staircase of development. This is called regression. A six-year-old might begin to wet his bed after many dry months. An eight-year-old might resume sucking her thumb.

A teenager might crawl in bed with Mom or Dad. These are natural and necessary coping mechanisms.

They are signs that more mature defenses have failed, so the child is retreating back to more primitive means of coping. There's no problem here, unless the regressed behavior gets in the way of healthy functioning (e.g., going to school, engaging peers, eating, sleeping, toileting) or persists long after the news.

What can a healthy parent do?
Help your kids manage their strong emotions by:

1 **Managing your own feelings.**
If you are calm, your kids will manage their emotions better.

2 **Labeling and validating their emotions.**
There is no "wrong" way to feel, even if there are unacceptable (and unsafe) ways to express those feelings.

3 **Making the news clear and predictable and concrete.**
What is happening when? Who will be where?

4 **Reassure your son or daughter that the things that are important to them will not change.**
Mom may be moving out on Friday, but we will still make sure that you get to soccer practice on Saturday and Kayla's birthday party on Sunday.

5 **Create a color-coded calendar.**
Review it every day in both homes. Yellow days are with Mom. Green days are with Dad.

6 **Rely on transitional objects.**
A transitional object is something that the child values that represents the absent parent. A stuffed animal. A locket. A photo. Spray the child's pajamas with your cologne so that she has your scent when she sleeps away at the other house. Tuck a note in her lunchbox or overnight bag.

Then it was just
me and Mom alone
in the big house.

The quiet scared me,
but Mom's crying
scared me more.

Mom asked me if I
could fill up the empty
space in the big bed.
The place where
Daddy used to sleep.

I still don't know if
that was more for me
or for her.

Whose Needs Are Being Served?

Today, we generally encourage parents to allow their children to remain children as long as possible.

I worry that this mother is asking Emma to fill in for her absent partner.

What do you think about Mom inviting Emma to fill the empty space in the big bed after Dad moved out? Was that kindness? Was that a loving parent's effort to anticipate the child's needs? Or was that self-serving? Was that Mom's wish to serve her own needs in the aftermath of a huge change?

It could be either or both, but I'm suspicious.

Emma didn't ask to sleep in the big bed. There's a good chance that the familiarity of sleeping in her own bed would reassure her.

Of course, Emma jumped at the chance, but you've got to wonder why. I suspect that part of the answer is that Emma wants to take care of Mom.

Certainly you've heard the stories about single mothers referring to their sons as "the man of the family." It may have been necessary to take the oldest son out of school so he could get a job back in the 1800s. Today, we generally encourage parents to allow their children to remain children as long as possible. I worry that this mother is asking Emma to fill in for her absent partner.

I still don't know...

How to be better prepared to understand and serve the needs of our kids?

NOT by drinking or drugging. NOT by overeating or gambling or escaping into video games. Those are short term solutions, at best, and more commonly become addictions that undermine parenting and mature functioning in general.

Choose a healthy diet and regular exercise. Keep current with your physician and dentist.

Join a group. Become involved in your community. Join a church, synagogue or mosque. Spend time among people who share your values, who support you, and who you can support.

Establish a trusting individual or group therapy with a skilled and trusted professional.

...I still don't know

We recognize three different ways that parents can undermine a child's childhood:

1 **An adultified child** is prematurely promoted to serve as a parent's ally, partner and friend. The adultified child is given adult-like privileges and access to adult information.

2 **A parentified child** is prematurely promoted to become a parent's caregiver, reversing roles entirely. The parentified child skips school and refuses playdates because *"Dad needs me."* She takes over responsibility for making sure that Mom takes her medicine or that Dad doesn't drink.

3 **An infantilized child** is forbidden from growing up because Mom or Dad needs to feel needed. This child will never have a playdate at a friend's house, will never go on a school field trip, and might not even go to school because the adult selfishly can't let go.

These distorted and pathological roles can feel good to children.

Adultified and parentified children are proud to be needed and valued by Mom or Dad. The infantilized child enjoys having every need catered to. All three might be vaguely aware of what they're missing, but the parent's needs are much more immediate and compelling. All three have stepped off the path of healthy development.

The problem should be obvious: Our job as parents is to serve our children's needs. Reversing that formula harms kids. That's not to say that adults don't have needs.

Of course we do. It's our responsibility to see that those needs are fulfilled in healthy adult-adult relationships so that we are better prepared to understand and serve the needs of our kids.

Daddy got the green
apartment. It was really
small and the walls were
bright, bright green.

We used to have lunch
together there every
Sunday. Daddy used to
let me spin on the bar
stools in the kitchen.

I remember how Daddy
would laugh and put potato
chips inside my peanut
butter and jelly sandwiches
to make them crunch...

"But I Only See Her Ten Hours a Week!"

No parent wants to miss out on events in their child's life.

Unfortunately, adult separation and divorce usually divide the child's time in two, allocating only a portion to each parent. That can mean that you will miss out on a lot.

It's tempting, therefore, to try to squeeze as much into the time that you have together as possible.

Homework? Chores? Rules?

It's easy to let those bothersome, time-consuming necessities go in favor of just plain having fun.

But it's selfish, too. This "Disney Land Dad" approach to parenting apart might serve your wish to be the good guy, free of the burdens of parenting, making her other parent into the bad guy. Fun in your home. Chores and homework, eat-your-vegetables and time-for-bed in the other home. If you love your child more than you hate her other parent, you'll put her needs first before your own.

She needs structure. She needs rules and schedules and boundaries so that she knows how to succeed, and she needs the confidence of knowing what will happen when she tests the limits (as every child must).

Here's the real test:

Which do you value more, your child's health or her happiness?

Happiness is fleeting. Happiness means giving her that third helping of dessert or giving in to her whining pleas to stay up late or ignoring the rules because you see her so seldom.

Her happiness selfishly saves you the trouble of setting limits and the pain of enduring her anger. It wins you the Momentary and superficial thrill of hearing that you're the best parent on Earth and the more-or-less implicit revenge of hearing how she loves you more than she loves her other parent.

Then he'd tell me not
to tell Mommy about
the crunchy sandwiches
because she'd get mad...

and we both knew
what happened when
Mommy got mad.

"Shhh!" he'd say.
"This is our special secret."

Valuing her health first and foremost means being firm and clear and following through. It means saying "no," and meaning it, and enduring her resulting tantrum. Valuing her health means helping her learn how to tolerate frustration and delay gratification and manage her emotions and control her impulses and play by the rules.

Valuing her health more than her happiness mean that she might sulk in her room screaming "*I hate you*" for those few short hours that she's in your care.

But because you're a good parent and a mature, healthy adult, you know that these Moments must happen, that discovering that her rage can be tolerated will help her mature, and that she loses far more than you might win by making yourself into the good parent.

Do you know what the most challenging health-versus-happiness choice is for any post-separation parent? When she resists or refuses spending time with her other parent.

Here are some thoughts:

1 **Beware that her resistance and your strong negative feelings about your ex- are connected.** Her resistance may be in part a wish to make you happy, in part a fear that spending time with the other parent is betraying you, and in part may feel like validation of your not-so-secret feelings about her other parent. Remember: she reads your feelings more easily than you are reading this page.

2 **Giving her the discretion to choose** whether to go may seem like the respectful thing to do or it may seem necessary because of her size, but neither is true. She needs the reassurance of knowing that the adults are in charge. You don't let her decide whether to go to school, do you?

3 **Communication is the key.** If she is having a problem with her other parent, they have to talk it out directly. Get yourself out of the middle.

4 **Absence does not make the heart grow fonder.**
The longer a parent and child are apart, the harder it will be to get them back together.

Change day
was dangerous.

I had one foot in
Mom-land and the
other foot in Dad-land.

Imagine going back and
forth between two
countries at war
three-times-a-week,
every week, forever.

That's what
it was like.

Making "Change Day" Easier On Everyone

Transitioning between separated caregivers can be **the hardest part** of a child's life.

The excitement and pleasure of seeing a parent after days apart is easily overcome by the expectation of renewed conflict. Bringing Mom and Dad together can feel like bringing a lit match close to a gallon of gasoline. Some children who seem to resist or refuse contact with their other parent are actually scared of the explosion that happens at transition.

They complain and tantrum and cry as transition approaches and especially while Mom and Dad are in the same room together, but they're fine once the adults are apart; once they've crossed the demilitarized zone back into safety.

I felt like
a traitor
every day.

I used to
forget:
where I was,
who I was...

...and
what I was
supposed to
do and say.

- What happens if school starts late, ends early or is cancelled for the day?
- Who is the parent-on-duty (that is, the parent responsible for Moment-to-Moment decision making) during the school day? This matters if, for example, the child is hurt on the playground at lunchtime.
- What to do with all the gear?
- Skis and ballet shoes and soccer balls?
- Should the sending parent deliver the gear to the receiving parent later, after the child is dropped at school?
- Will the school hold the gear until dismissal?
- Should the parents jointly rent a self-storage locker in between the two homes for this purpose?

The answer will require that you clarify either that the sending parent remains the parent on duty until school dismissal, or that the receiving parent assumes responsibility upon the child's arrival on school grounds. (I generally find that the former plan makes more practical sense.)

When "change day" is difficult

These plans can save everyone a lot of grief,
as long as you've planned ahead:

1   **Make the details familiar and predictable.** When transition happens at one of the parents' homes, establish a routine. For example, agree that the "sending parent" (the parent ending a period of care) always drives and transition occurs at the "receiving parent's" (the parent beginning a period of care) front door.

2   If transition at either or both homes is forbidden by the courts or feels threatening or awkward to anyone involved, **transition should occur at a neutral, public place.** Choose some place comfortable without a lot of distractions. A local grocery store or fast food restaurant parking lot might work.

3   **Script the transition for the adults.** This is not the time or place to try to communicate anything. That communication should happen just before or just after transition, so that the receiving parent is up-to-date on the child's needs and well-being. The adults' words at transition should be rote and said with a smile: *"Hi Joe. How are you?" "Fine Mary, thanks. How are you?" "I'm good. Thanks. Emma, say hi to your Dad. Have a good time you guys. See you in three days!"* End of dialogue. Sending parent exits stage left.

4   And if those clues aren't enough, if "change day" continues to spark anxiety and upset for all involved- **consider transitioning through a neutral third party** (or agency) so that the adults need not come face-to-face. Many parenting plans require that the sending parent drop the child at school in the morning and the receiving parent collect the child from school in the afternoon. Sometimes the same thing can be accomplished through the child's therapy hour.

At first, I felt like
an ostrich.

Ostriches bury their
heads in the sand
when they're
scared so they can't
see or hear what
scares them.

Denial, Minimization, and Escape

Imagine this: Open African savannah. An ostrich and a leopard. The ostrich sees the leopard, and does what ostriches do.

He buries his head in the sand. He pretends that if he can't see the threat, it isn't there. That's denial. Pretending that something obvious isn't real. *Mom and Dad are not fighting. Divorce? No one said anything about divorce!*

The ostrich's denial works, but only for a Moment. Denial is a very short-term, very immature way of protecting yourself from pain. You know what happens Moments later, right? Nature takes its course. The leopard has lunch. The ostrich might live a bit longer if he convinced himself that leopard is just a baby. Not a serious threat, right? *I can outrun him. And if he catches me, I can fight him off.* Minimization makes something big and scary less threatening. Minimization is slightly more adaptive than denial.

Sometimes minimization can help us get used to the full impact of a threat one tiny bit at a time.

I know what you're thinking: *Escape! That's the answer.* The ostrich should pump his long, powerful legs as hard as he can and get the heck off the savannah. True, if this were really a nature documentary, that is the big bird's best chance for survival. It's also the coping mechanism too many of us use far too often.

Human escape comes in the form of drugs and alcohol and video games. Workaholic and perfectionistic and over-eating and other addictive behaviors—and sleep.

"Everything is fine!"
I told grandma and
my teachers and my
friends or

"Leave me alone" or

"I don't want to
talk about it!"

The truth is that running away is just another short-term solution. The problem might disappear for days or weeks or even years, but its not gone. And the damage done along the way is never worth it.

Kids use denial and minimization and escape to cope with family conflict, adult separation and divorce. The reality is just as scary as the leopard is to the ostrich, so they cope as best as they can.

There's no way to make these realities painless. Trying to do so is lying. That's your guilt-induced effort to hide your head in the sand. What we must do, instead, is make the pain as manageable as possible, make sure that our kids don't make choices that compound the pain (like drinking and drugging), and be there to comfort and reassure our kids as they come to grips with the pain.

How to make the pain as manageable as possible?

1 If you must argue in front of your kids, **be sure to make up in front of them,** too. Teach them through your example that anger is manageable and is part of a loving relationship.

2 **Never pull your kids into the conflict.** It is simply selfish and abusive to damn your daughter's other parent to or around your kids. Rather than, "did you see how crazy she is?" try, "Sorry. I bet seeing that's confusing. Your Mom and I need to figure this stuff out."

3 **Give your kids one consistent, non-blaming, non-shaming message** about what's happening. Different explanations from Mom and Dad will only make things worse.

4 **Safety first!** If you believe that your son or daughter is using substances, is depressed (often associated with sleep changes), is self-destructive (e.g., cutting herself) or suicidal, reach out for help now. Dial 9-1-1. Take her to the local hospital emergency room. Find a trusted therapist. Check in with the pediatrician.

It didn't take me long
to figure it all out.

Anger broke your love.
Our family was ending.

I didn't know
what to do.

I learned to
change my colors
like a chameleon.

Is Anger the Opposite of Love?

No. Anger is part of a loving relationship, just like happiness, sadness and fear.

Love is the safety net that makes having and expressing those natural and necessary human experiences acceptable.

The problem is that children who see anger end adult love, fear that anger is unacceptable, dangerous and scary.

They fear that *if anger ended my parents' love, then my anger might end my parent's love for me, too.*

Living with this fear and misconception turns children into chameleons. Rather than have your own thoughts and feelings, these children change their emotional colors to fit in to the environment.

Weekends with Mom? Say and do what Mom wants to hear and see. That way she smiles and hugs me and gets me good stuff. That way she loves me. If that means cursing about Dad, who cares? Dad will never know, right?

Weekdays with Dad? Say and do what Dad needs to hear and see. That way he smiles and hugs me and gets me good stuff. That way he loves me. If that means cursing about Mom, then who cares? Mom will never know, right?

Right? Mom will never know that I'm damning her to Dad, and Dad will never know that I'm damning him to Mom, because Mom and Dad never talk to each other.

So what's the problem?

I said to Dad what
I knew Dad wanted
to hear, I said to Mom
what I knew Mom
wanted to hear.

Because you didn't
talk to each other,
you never knew that
my words were just
echoes of your own.

Having my own feelings
was too dangerous.

Becoming a chameleon sounds like a terrific solution! **NOPE. There's at least two very serious problems:**

Mom and Dad each talk to their lawyers. The lawyers file motions and go to court. The judge gets confused when the two lawyers BOTH say that Emma wants to only live with his or her client. The judge gets even more confused when Mom's lawyer reports that Emma told Mom that Dad hurts her, or when Dad's lawyer reports that Emma told Dad that Mom neglects her. The legal process spins up, child protective services get called, Guardians ad litem are appointed, therapists are hired, and huge amounts of money are spent all because Emma is just trying to be loved by both of her parents.

What is a chameleon's real color? There's no way to know because they always adapt to the color of the setting that they're in. That works if you're a lizard. If you're a child, changing your colors to win love is a great short-term adaptation that can cause a terrible long-term outcome. The chameleon child is at risk of growing up without knowing herself. She'll struggle to be independent and is at very high risk of getting into unhealthy, overly dependent relationships.

So, **what's the solution?**

Chameleon children need both permission and experience having their own thoughts and feelings. They need instruction and examples of how to think for yourself, how to express a strong feeling, and they need emotional support to manage the terror that those expressions will cost them love.

Healthy parents help children manage this experience beginning in infancy and especially through the experience of adult separation and divorce.

When parents can't or don't provide this experience, children will need impartial professional helpers: School counselors, skilled clergy, conscientious and caring coaches, and/or trusted therapists.

More than just rules and direction, these kids need long term relationships in which anger can erupt and be managed safely, without loss of love.

Sometimes you
made me deliver stuff
back and forth.

Mail that came to
the wrong address.

Child support checks.
Lawyer papers.

Angry notes
and letters.

Parent-Parent Communications

Don't make the kids into your messengers. Find better ways to communicate directly and constructively and proactively with your children's other parent.

Here's a true story:
Billy's mother was in the habit of tucking letters to Billy's Dad in Billy's backpack when she sent him off to school on "change days." Billy was young. If he even knew the letters were there, he didn't care. Dad routinely went through Billy's backpack at the end of each school so that homework would get done and he stayed current on the million notices the school sent home most weeks.

Discovering the materials sent from Mom was never pleasant, but the system worked more-or-less, until one Wednesday in spring.

Wednesday was Billy's "change day." Mom dropped him at school. Dad picked him up after school. This was the first warm day after months of winter cold, so Billy hung out with his friends on the playground before school.

His friends saw Mom's notes in Billy's backpack, grabbed them and ran. Pretty soon, everyone knew what Billy's Mom thought about Billy's Dad.

Here's another: Dad asked Sally to give Mom an envelope at every transition. Sally did what she was told, but every time she got in Mom's car and Mom opened the envelope, Mom yelled at her: *"How can he think….?* or *"I can't believe that he….!"* or *"Where's my check, Sally? If Daddy didn't give us a check then we can't get food this weekend!"*

The moral of these stories must be clear: Emma's experience is not unique.
Don't make the kids into your messengers.

At first I felt special,
like you trusted me.

Then I peeked.
I saw what you sent
to each other.

That's when I started
to hate being your
messenger.

Why couldn't you
talk to each other?

Find better ways to communicate with your children's other parent

Directly, constructively, and proactively. For example:

1   **The low-tech solution** is a paper and pen record that goes back and forth at the time of transition directly from one adult hand into another. Structure the format so that the communication is routine and focused.

Each entry should provide succinct, factual updates in distinct areas of functioning such as school, eating, sleeping, toileting, friends, extra-curriculars and health.

Try not to focus only on problems by adding a category for **successes and matters of pride.**

2   **The high tech solution communicates the same information (and more) online.** Make sure that you use an encrypted and password protected platform and, like with the paper notebook, make sure that the kids don't have access.

3   **Better still? Talk to each other.** Get over the anger and grief and pain. Recognize that the kids' needs come first, then pick up the phone or make a date to meet over coffee and talk. Should you bring your new partners?

Maybe. Talk about that, too. Be clear about the ground rules: If anyone feels uncomfortable or unsafe, or if the conversation ceases to be constructive, you'll stop. Period.

Here are some popular tools to consider:

www.ourfamilywizard.com
www.sharekids.com/
www.womansdivorce.com/parenting-plan-calendar.html
www.coparentpro.com
www.highconflictinstitute.com/biff-responses

You never trusted
each other.
So you taught me
how to be your spy.

You taught me how
to snoop and sneak
and keep secrets...
and I was good at it.

Keeping Kids Out of the Middle

Human beings are like cars. **We all need emotional fuel.** Healthy adults refuel one another. Parents refuel children.

When an adult relationship fails, healthy men and woman find other healthy adults to refuel them: Siblings, neighbors, friends, co-workers, your local clergy-person, your doctor, and/or a trusted therapist.

It's painful and disorienting to change from one familiar gas station to others, but it's necessary because everyone needs emotional fuel to survive.

Parents, in particular, need to keep their tanks full so that they can refuel their kids.

The problem is that some parents become so caught up in the adult conflict, that they ask their children to refuel them. They enlist their kids like peers to validate their position in the adult conflict. They enlist them as spies.

The plan is "brilliant." Only your son or daughter can get so close to the other adult without raising suspicion.

Who else could wander around your ex's new apartment, intercept his email and text messages? Who else could report in about whether he's dating? About how much he's drinking? Who else could gather all the dirt that your lawyer needs to win the case? To get you full custody? To prove to the world that you were right to reject the jerk?

Chances are that your daughter will be glad to help. She'll be thrilled to feel trusted and needed and valuable. She'll drink up the love and affection and attention and praise that you offer when she comes back with more news because you are her fuel tank.

Did you even know
that I read the text
messages on your
phones and your
emails when you
weren't looking?

You made it pretty
clear that I had to
pick sides.

She'd do almost anything to get that emotional fuel, even betray her other parent. Even take sides in the adult war.

Enlisting your child as your spy is a "brilliant" plan, except that it's entirely selfish and abusive.

Asking your child to take sides, to betray her other parent, to lie and deceive and sneak and steal is far worse than bad modeling and direction. You'd do less damage if you taught her how to shoplift, because shoplifting doesn't create a loyalty conflict deep within her budding sense of self. This plan does, so don't.

Let me explain:
You and your child's other parent each donated twenty-three chromosomes that came together to create your child.

I've called her Emma. In a very similar manner, you and Emma's other parent both contribute half of her emerging sense of self.

Some of your behaviors, ideas, beliefs and interests plus some of your co-parent's behaviors, ideas, beliefs and interests lay the foundation of herself.

The quality of your adult relationship becomes the bond that holds the two growing parts of Emma's self together, deep in her psyche.

That's why the legal status of your relationship doesn't matter, but your mutual ability to communicate and cooperate and be consistent matters a lot.

When the adult relationship fails, a fault line appears in the foundation of your child's self—a crack. She can grow and mature for a hundred years without any serious problems with that crack deep inside herself, or you can drive a wedge into it.

You can selfishly force her to reject part of herself. By doing so, you might feel briefly validated, but she will live every day feeling torn in two.

All I ever wanted
was a family like
I saw on TV...

Fantasies of the Intact Family Persist

Children long for their broken families to reunite days and weeks and months and years and long decades after a split.

Two things continue to astonish me in my work as a psychotherapist, even after thirty-plus years:

The **first** are the incredibly brave and resilient adults who live through horrific abuses in their childhoods but somehow go on to become healthy parents themselves. I find this to be a miraculous testament to the buoyance of the human spirit and evidence of real goodness in a world that has far too little of it.

The **second** thing that never fails to astonish me in my work as a psychologist is the stubborn persistence of the wish for an intact family.

It doesn't matter whether the child is three-years-old and struggling ostrich-like to cope with yesterday's news, or seventy-three-years-old reminiscing about childhood. It really is as if Mom and Dad each contribute half of who we each become and the idea of breaking that whole in two can never genuinely be grasped.

Sure, we can gradually come to understand that the adult relationship ended, but understanding is cognitive. It's in our brains. The fantasy of the intact family lives on in our hearts.

Does that mean that you should never divorce? Does it mean that you should stay in a bad relationship long after all other reasonable remedies have failed? No. Of course not.

The damage done to a child who is forced to spend her life living in a war zone is much, much worse.

like the
other
kids
talked
about.

Guide your parenting choices:

By knowing that your kids might always nurture a wish for you and their other parent to get back together.

1 **Listen for this theme and give it a voice.** When Emma told her Mom that it was "weird" seeing her parents standing together on the sidelines at the soccer game, Mom had a chance to clarify the feeling (*"what kind of weird, sweetie?"*), to validate it (*"I'm sure it made you happy and sad, both"*) and to normalize it (*"Do you know that lots of kids whose parents are apart wish that they were back together?"*).

2 **Don't fall for denial:** *"Yuck! It was horrible when you guys were together! I don't want that again!"* Chances are that underneath the "yuck" and even though she knows that you're remarried, and Dad has a girlfriend, and you live in different states, that fantasy lingers deep down anyway.

3 **Watch out for the "parent trap."** Some kids want to engineer an adult reunion the way that a pair of twins tried in a well-known movie. If you see a parent trap ahead, be grateful but be clear. Acknowledge the idea: *"Honey, that's the nicest thing."* Validate the motivating emotion: *"I know you wish we never broke up."* But be clear: *"That won't work sweetie. Mommy and I aren't going to get back together."*

4 **Reassure. This is critically important.** The script goes like this:"Once upon a time Daddy and I met and fell in love and we made you. We loved each other. Mommy loved you and I loved you. Adult love can stop, and ours has. Parent-child love can never stop, and ours won't. Now Mommy and Daddy don't love each other anymore, but Daddy will always love you and I will always love you, too."

5 **Lose the guilt immediately!** Your wishy-washy statements or your abstract *"Well I still love him, just not that way"* or your lingering hope (*"Maybe someday..."*) will only confuse your kids. If the adult relationship is done, it's done. Your job is to gently, lovingly help your kids come to terms with that change and move on

Every time you went
back to court...
There was a new
Guardian or doctor
or lawyer to talk to.

They all asked nosy
questions and
made me promises
they couldn't keep.

Blah   Blah

                Blah

The Best Interests of the Child? [BIC]

Beware of the Legal System!
Our courts were designed to judge **guilt versus innocence.**

Many judges and lawyers approach family law as if there must be one good guy and one bad guy. That might work in a murder trial or on TV, but family matters aren't about right and wrong.

Family law isn't black or white. All cases are all gray and they're all about understanding and serving the needs of the kids.

When separation, divorce and post-divorce conflicts (e.g., requests to move out of state or to adjust the schedule of care) end up in court, the court is responsible for determining "the Best Interests of the Child" (or the BIC).

Because judges can't climb down off the bench, set aside their gavels and come over after school to talk to your kids, different courts have invented different ways of evaluating the BIC.

"This will be over soon"

Blah

"I'll make sure you get what you want"

Blah

"This isn't your fault."

Yeah, right...

Blah

You may be able to use **less adversarial means** of resolving adult differences. Depending on your jurisdiction, these may include:

Mediation/arbitration. Meeting with a skilled professional to help you find middle ground. Sometimes children have an opportunity to be heard in this process.

Collaborative law. This is a very specific alternative legal process. Specially trained "collaborative" lawyers work together to reach mutual, child-centered outcomes.

Parenting Coordination. Skilled legal or mental health professionals are appointed by the court to meet with co-parents to use education, mediation and—when necessary—arbitration to settle child-centered disputes within the parameters of the existing parenting plan..

Ways of evaluating the BIC

Which of these (or other alternatives) are available to you will depend on where you are and the specifics of your child's situation.

1

A Guardian ad litem (GAL)
Will be appointed to serve as the judge's eyes and ears. Typically the court will appoint a specially trained attorney or mental health professional to answer specific questions about the child, the child's relationship with each parent and in both homes. Some GALs are responsible to advise the court about the child's needs. Others are responsible to report the child's wishes.

2

A custody evaluator
Is a specially trained mental health professional who will interview both parents, the child, observe the parent-child and parent-parent interactions, collect history and speak with references and may conduct psychological testing.

3

A child's attorney
Might be available to interview the child and advise the court about the child's needs, wishes and maturity. Maturity is frequently used to determine how much weight the child's wishes should be given.

4

Voice of the child evaluations
A skilled professional interviews the child and advises the court about the child's wishes, needs and maturity.

5

A child protective worker, child advocate or CASA volunteer
may be involved when questions about safety arise.

Unfortunately, the court's usual methods of getting at the BIC can exacerbate the adult conflict. The trickle-down tension can make the situation harder for the kids.

I really didn't need
to know about court.

But you showed me
the papers and told
me everything.

You said that
I deserved to know,
because it was all
"about me"...

→ TMI!

Too Much Information.

Don't hide behind the excuse that you're *"just telling her the truth"* or *"she deserves to know, it's about her"* or *"she's old enough—she gets it."*

Here's what your children **NEED TO KNOW** every day from all of their caregivers:	You are safe.
	You are loved.
	Your thoughts and feelings matter.
	Your job is to be the child.
	My job is to be the parent. Your other parent and I are learning how to work together to make sure that you're okay.
	You have two homes now.
	When you're in my care, I get to make the rules. When you're in your other parent's care, s/he gets to make the rules.
...when you're in my care: (whether we're together or apart)	You can always say what you think and how you feel as long as you are polite and respectful.
	The rules are: _____ [Fill in the blank: Curfew? Bedtime? Chores?].
	Here's how you can earn privileges, goodies, and respect: _____ [The answer here can be different for each child according to his/her abilities and needs].
	Here's how you risk losing privileges, goodies, and respect: _____ [The answer here can be different for each child according to his/her abilities and needs].
	Your schedule will generally look like this: [Fill in the blank]. There will be exceptions and I will expect you to be flexible.

You even asked me
to choose: Did I want
to live with Mommy
or with Daddy?

Don't you get it?

That's like asking
you whether you
want to cut off
your left arm or your
right arm.

It's an
impossible choice.

Here's what your children **DO NOT** need to know and **SHOULD NOT** hear or see.

(This includes protecting your children from peeking at your electronic communications, overhearing your spoken communications and locking away your paperwork.)

Anything that damns, diminishes or otherwise denigrates their other parent or any caregiver. Regardless of that person's legal status, geographic location, skin color, gender, sexual orientation, religion, size, shape or national origin.

Model respect and value diversity. Put your feelings aside: Don't you want your child to have as many supports and as much love in this world as possible?

Details of your adult conflict. Unless and until either (a) you and the child's other parent mutually decide what to say and how to say it, and/or (b) a child-centered established authority (e.g., a judge, the GAL) instructs you to share specific information and how.

Your adult fears and worries, pain and rage. That doesn't mean smile and lie. The kids can know that this is hard time, but need to be reassured that you have adult helpers and that you will be okay.

That you aren't emotionally available to help them with their needs. If you must be absent and unavailable via distance media (for example, if there's a restraining order), make sure that they know that you're okay, who will be available for them while you're away, and when you'll return.

Now that
I've graduated,
maybe you think
it's over.

True, I'm an
"adult" now.

Your selfish war
shouldn't matter
to me anymore.
I wish that was true.

I'm still your child.
I always will be.

Childhood Does Not End at 18 Years Old

Eighteen is an arbitrary landmark. It is NOT the case that we go to sleep on the last day of our seventeenth year and wake up transformed the next morning. Maturity is a gradual process of growing up that unfolds uniquely for each of us.

Your kids' daughter's birthday is not like the timer going off on the microwave or that little button popping up on the Thanksgiving turkey. Eighteen does not mean "done" or "mature" or ready to manage adult stress, even if it may mean voting rights and responsibilities. But you rationalize that she's an adult, now: *"I can tell her what really happened!"*

True, on her six thousand, five hundred and seventieth day since birth the law says that she's no longer a minor, but psychology says she's still a child and always will be your child. Even when she's forty-five.

She still needs to feel free to love and be loved by whomever she chooses without being torn apart or emotionally crippled by loyalty binds. She still needs the security of knowing that you and her other parent can put aside your differences and work together to catch her when she falls. That's what healthy parents do when their five-year-old falls off her bicycle, when their sixteen-year-old gets her heart broken by a boy, when their twenty-year-old gets fired from a job, and even when the forty-year-old needs emergency surgery.

A lot changes over the years. Our kids develop a more coherent sense of self. They learn how to manage their bodies and their emotions. They build relationships outside of home in clubs and on teams, with friends and with intimate partners. They develop strengths and weaknesses, fears and hopes, goals and dreams, and they learn from their failures.

I still feel like a traitor
when I have to choose
whose house to visit
first, or where to
spend the holidays.

But mostly I'm scared
I'll make the same
mistakes that you did.

I'm scared that if I ever
have kids of my own,
that I'll be just as
selfish as you are.

Intergenerational patterns

But even after all of this, they still need you as a parent

This means:

1 **Don't set up her eighteenth birthday as a magic date when all doors previously sealed will automatically burst open**, bathing the child in the shining light of truth. You're still her parent. You and her other parent still need to protect her, and she still needs to respect your privacy.

2 **Don't set up 18-years-old as a magic date when she'll suddenly be entitled to make all of her own decisions**, particularly if she lives with you, if she drives your car, or if she's on your medical insurance. She may legally be released to go where she pleases, when she pleases, but you and her other parent still have rules and expectations.

3 **Work with your co-parent to gradually give her more responsibility and greater privileges as she approaches eighteen.** Watch carefully how she manages those freedoms. If you give her too much and she falls down, take a step back. If she succeeds, consider giving her a bit more up to and beyond age eighteen.

4 If you feel an urge to share previously sensitive adult information with your young adult kids, **start by asking yourself whose need you're serving?** If it's your need to feel validated or vindicated, or your need to finally be seen as the good parent, stop. It's not your child's job to serve your needs, whether she's eight or eighteen or eighty.

5 **What does she expect to learn? How would it affect her?** If your child is chomping at the bit, eager to FINALLY learn the truth—whatever that may mean—take a step back and figure out why she's so eager.

I love you, Mom.
I love you, Dad.

And I know that
you both love me as
well as you know how.

Love should never
mean taking sides.

If you love me more
than you hate each
other, my happiness
will be more important
to you than bickering
over money and control
and power.

If you love me more than you hate each other, you will find a way to work together to parent me even though your adult relationship has ended.

If you love me more than you hate each other, then you will never ask me to choose between you, you will never damn my other parent.

You will never make
me into your messenger
or your spy.

You will never force me
to become a chameleon
or allow me to bury my
head in the sand like
an ostrich.

If you love me more
than you hate each
other, you will never
put me in the middle.

Benjamin D. Garber, PhD

is a New Hampshire licensed psychologist. He serves the needs of children whose parents are conflicted, separated and divorced as a child and family therapist, custody evaluator, parenting coordinator, expert witness and formerly as a Guardian ad litem. Dr. Garber provides advance training to family law professionals in all matters related to understanding and serving the needs of children.

He is a prolific, award-winning author.

Dr. Garber's website is **www.healthyparent.com**

Other books by Dr. Garber	Holding Tight/Letting Go (2015)
	The Roadmap to the Parenting Plan Worksheet (2015)
	Ten Child-Centered Forensic Family Evaluation Tools (2015)
	Developmental Psychology for Family Law Professionals (2009)
	Keeping Kids Out of the Middle (2008)
	Healthy Parenting Series 1. The Healthy Parent's ABCs (2015) 2. Caught in the Middle (2019) 3. Taming the Beast (2019)

Resources that Can Help

Keeping kids out of the middle

Keeping Kids Out Of The Middle:
Parenting Effectively In The Midst
Of Adult Conflict, Separation and Divorce.
Benjamin D. Garber

Putting Children First:
Proven Parenting Strategies for Helping
Children Thrive Through Divorce.
JoAnne Pedro-Carroll

Two Homes, One Childhood:
A Parenting Plan to Last a Lifetime
Robert E. Emery

Divorce Poison New and Updated Edition:
How to Protect Your Family from Bad-mouthing
and Brainwashing
Richard A Warshak

Creating parenting plans

The Roadmap to The Parenting Plan Worksheet
Benjamin D. Garber

The Parenting Plan Workbook:
A Comprehensive Guide to Building a Strong,
Child-Centered Parenting Plan
Karen Bonnell

Parenting Plans For Families After Divorce
Joan H. McWilliams

Co-parenting

Parenting Without Conflict Online Course
12 sessions for parents and 4 sessions for parents and kids

Bill Eddy

Shared Parenting Workbook:
Sharing-parenting after Divorce – What is it, how does it
work and will it work for you?

Toby Hazlewood

The Co-Parenting Handbook:
Raising Well-Adjusted and Resilient Kids from Little
Ones to Young Adults through Divorce or Separation

Karen Bonnell

The Co-Parenting Survival Guide:
Letting Go of Conflict After a Difficult Divorce

Elizabeth Thayer and Jeffrey Zimmerman

Co-Parenting Works!:
Helping Your Children Thrive after Divorce

Tammy G Daughtry

BIFF: Quick Responses to High-Conflict People,
Their Personal Attacks, Hostile Email and Social Media
Meltdowns

Bill Eddy

Mom's House, Dad's House:
Making two homes for your child

Isolina Ricci

Healthy parenting

Holding Tight/Letting Go:
Raising Healthy Kids in Anxious Times.

Benjamin D. Garber

Talking to Children About Divorce:
A Parent's Guide to Healthy Communication at Each Stage
of Divorce: Expert Advice for Kids' Emotional Recovery

Jean McBride

Collateral Damage: Guiding and Protecting
Your Child Through the Minefield of Divorce

John Chirban

Also in the **Healthy Parenting** series:

The Healthy Parent's ABCs
Benjamin Garber PhD

Twenty-six letters. Twenty-six lessons. Caregiving environments, schools and child-centered organizations assign one letter per week to complete the alphabet in full twice each year!

This fun little book is a simple "how to" guide for new parents. It is intended to be a quick and easy way to get professional parenting advice in small bites! *The Healthy Parent's ABCs* is parenting made simple. Laid out in twenty-six sections corresponding to the letters of the English alphabet, couples, groups or classes can move from one lesson to the next, one letter at a time. It's an entire curriculum for anyone!

Taming the Beast: Managing Anger in Ourselves and Our Children Through Divorce
Benjamin Garber PhD

We all get mad sometimes, but out-of-control anger can make life miserable for everyone, especially during family breakups.

In *Taming the Beast*, Dr. Benjamin Garber shows parents and kids how to understand anger in all its forms, from irritation to frustration to rage, and express it constructively using the MadMeter™.

With practice, you and your kids will discover healthy ways to experience your own emotions—and accept each other's.

CPSIA information can be obtained
at www.ICGtesting.com
Printed in the USA
JSHW010019310123
36981JS00001B/1

9 781950 057221